T0198962

God's Will
for *Abundant*
LIFE

Study Guide

REV. MILTON L. SEAMON

Balboa Press books may be ordered through booksellers or by contacting:

Balboa Press
A Division of Hay House
1663 Liberty Drive
Bloomington, IN 47403
www.balboapress.com
1 (877) 407-4847

Because of the dynamic nature of the Internet, any web addresses or links contained in this book may have changed since publication and may no longer be valid. The views expressed in this work are solely those of the author and do not necessarily reflect the views of the publisher, and the publisher hereby disclaims any responsibility for them.

Any people depicted in stock imagery provided by Getty Images are models, and such images are being used for illustrative purposes only.
Certain stock imagery © Getty Images.

Scripture taken from the King James Version of the Bible.

ISBN: 978-1-9822-4595-5 (sc)
ISBN: 978-1-9822-4594-8 (e)

Print information available on the last page.

Balboa Press rev. date: 04/02/2020

BALBOA.PRESS

To Milton L. Seamon Sr., who told me at an early age about Christ. And to my mother, Mayola Seamon, who fought all her battles on her knees. Last, but not least, to my aunt Ruth, who kept a Bible at arm's reach at all times.

Rest in paradise.

Introduction

I've read such books as *Think and Grow Rich,* which is an awesome book.

But I have a text that is even better to renew your mind for abundant life: Romans 12:2. Amen!

Or here's another one: *Rich Dad Poor Dad.* It also is an awesome book.

But again, I have one even better: our Heavenly Father is as rich as it gets (Psalm 50:10; Haggai 2:8; Ezekiel 28:13). Amen!

So you see, all this and more are His, and because we are His heirs, we share in His will for abundant life.

Lesson 1

PART 1

Abundance

God wants us as Christians to live abundantly. Amen.
God's Word tells us (Romans 12:2; John 10:10; Matthew 6:10). Amen.

As Christians, we serve a God of abundance and not a god of little, although He says if we only had faith the size of a mustard seed. Let's keep in mind that this is a small seed that produces a large plant (Luke 17:6). Amen.

God wants to bless us (Malachi 3:10; Psalm 50:10; Haggai 2:8). Amen!

How can we serve a God of abundance when we have no faith or trust in God's Word? Elshaddai means "God Almighty."

God gave us His only begotten Son because He loves us (John 3:16). So why wouldn't He give us whatever else we need?

Read 1 Peter 2:24. Amen. I tell you when Jesus died, was buried, and rose on that third day, He took our sins away.

God the Father and His Son, Lord Jesus Christ, with the helper the Holy Spirit, let us live an abundant life (Philippians 4:13). Amen.

Three Ingredients for Abundant Life

- God
- God's Word (John 1:1)
- You putting it in action

I pray that this lesson and scripture in abundance will bless your lives.

In Jesus's name, thank You, God.
Amen.

Lesson 1

PART 2

Abundance

2 Corinthian 9:8

God is able to do His part. I'll even take it a step farther and say it's already been done (John 19:30). Amen.

Ephesians 3:20 tells us God is more than able and beyond what we can imagine. Philippians 4:13 tells us that we can do all things through Christ, who strengthens us. Amen. Not some things but all things. So that includes living life abundantly.

Our Part

According to Mark 11:22, Jesus answered them by telling them to have faith in God. Jesus said we can move mountains when we have faith and don't doubt.

One time I was praying Psalm 23:4—"Yea though I walk through the valley of the shadow of doubt"—then I said, "I'm sorry, Lord. I mean *death*. And God said to me, "No, you're right. Doubt is death spiritually."

And besides that, it's only a shadow. Trust me: that's what God is telling us. Proverbs 3:5–6 says to lean not on your own in all your ways. There is that word *all* again! It still means *all*.

When we submit to Him, God will make our path straight, meaning we will be able to move that mountain. So when we trust in the Lord and commit, His light will shine in us (Psalm 37:5–6). So we should say Psalm 13:5.

God, I pray this lesson and scripture on abundance. And I trust You will bless our lives in Jesus's name. Thank You. Amen.

Lesson 2

Abundant Life: God Shall Supply

Philippians 4:19 says, "My God shall supply all." There is that word *all* again. Your needs through His riches in glory, Jesus. You see, if we seek Him first, who is *Him?* God! Amen (Matthew 6:19–24).

Whose team are you on? Some folks talk about straddling the fence. God said in Matthew 6:25–34 to not worry. It sounds like a command, and if you don't see it that way, it's okay. I'm sure we will agree that's an instruction. Amen (Deuteronomy 7:9). So we should keep His commandments (Malachi 3:10).

God wants to pour out a blessing of abundance on our lives more than we can wrap our minds around (Isaiah 55:8–9). Amen.

The God we serve is awesome. I say this even when we screw up (Isaiah 55:7; Job 12:5).

This verse tells me I need to mimic Jesus and not the world and the things in it (Luke 12:15) because we are not citizens of the world. Our citizenship is where our Lord and Savior lives, which is in heaven (Philippians 3:20). Amen.

God, I pray that through this lesson of scriptures on abundance, You will supply, and You will bless our lives.

In Jesus's name, I thank You.
Amen.

Lesson 3

Abundant Life: We Must Be Servants like Jesus

The problem is that we want and want, but first, we need to give! To give our time, talents, and tithes as Christians. Amen.

Philippians 2:3–8 says when we became Christians, we became servants like Jesus, but the only way this can happen is we *must die* to self. Jesus died for our sins and we get saved (John 3:30). Amen. What Jesus said in Mark 9:35 makes me think of when I was a kid and if you cut the line, you were told to go to the end.

I don't know about you, but I strive to be like the Lord, and the only way is to become a servant of the Lord. Amen.

That means we can no longer put ourselves first because it's putting ourselves last. Amen (Matthew 20:27–28).

According to John 13:3–5, Jesus leads by the example that God, His Father, gave! Read John 3:16. Jesus has taught us how to serve. Amen (John 13:12–15).

I pray that this lesson and scripture on being a servant of the Lord will bless your life. Thank you in Jesus's name. Amen.

Lesson 4

Abundant Life: Faith

What a man sows shall he reap, says Galatians 6:7. In this case, a woman imagined the faith that she had (Matthew 9:18–22). Jesus also raised the girl from the dead because of the faith her father had (Matthew 15:21–28). Come on, men. Here is another woman of great faith (John 11:21–27).

So now that we know what faith looks like, we need patience because they go hand in hand (Isaiah 40:31; Romans 8:24–25). We must be patient, knowing that whatever we ask God for, we will get in Jesus's name (Matthew 21:22).

So waiting on the Lord does make us stronger in Him, as God the Father, Jesus the Son, and the Holy Spirit, our interpreter, instruct us (Psalm 37:7).

So in other words, don't worry about what the Joneses are doing and how they are living. Wait for your word from the Lord. Please believe that if you are faithful, patient, and obedient, God will bless you. Also keep in mind Romans 2:11. Amen.

I pray that this lesson and scripture on faith and patience will bless your life.

Thank you in Jesus's name.
Amen.

Lesson 5

Abundant Life: Obedience

Read James 2:14–26. The Bible says without faith, work is dead. So we have determined that faith is a key element for our part.

So now let's look at obedience. We have been told as children to honor our mothers and fathers and our days shall be lengthened (Ephesians 6:1–3). Just as we think our children love us and respect us, they will obey us and the Heavenly Father and Son the same way.

According to John 15:14 and 1 Samuel 15:22, God gave His only Son, Jesus, so that we don't have to sacrifices lambs. Jesus said all we have to do is have faith (Matthew 8:26).

Here are some scriptures for loss of blessing for disobedience:

- Number 20:7–12
- Joshua 5:6
- Romans 2:6–8

But we can't forget how we got in this predicament: Adam's disobedience (Genesis 3:1–13).

I pray that this lesson in obedience will bless your life. Thank you in Jesus's name. Amen.

Lesson 6

Abundant Blessing: The Fruit from Being Obedient

In lesson 5, we looked at a loss of blessing by being disobedient. Now let's look at the rewards for being obedient.

Genesis 22:17–18	Proverbs 13:13
Psalm 1:1–2	Luke 11:28
John 14:15–21	1 John 5:3
Psalm 119:44	Psalm 119:59
Psalm 112:1	Exodus 23:22
Matthew 9:9	John 8:51
Hebrew 11:17	Matthew 6:24
Acts 23:1	James 1:22–25

I pray that this lesson in scriptures will bless your life.
Thank you in Jesus's name. Amen.

Don't forget it's a blessing to be a blessing (Acts 20:35).

Be blessed.

Printed in the United States
By Bookmasters